The Living Waters Between Us

The Living Waters Between Us

Poems by

Kathryn Ridall

© 2025 Kathryn Ridall. All rights reserved.
This material may not be reproduced in any form, published,
reprinted, recorded, performed, broadcast,
rewritten or redistributed without
the explicit permission of Kathryn Ridall.
All such actions are strictly prohibited by law.

Cover design by Shay Culligan
Cover image: "Ovation" by Rebecca Rivers
Author photo by Roger Barry

ISBN: 978-1-63980-799-4

Kelsay Books
502 South 1040 East, A-119
American Fork, Utah 84003
Kelsaybooks.com

for Roger

Acknowledgments

My gratitude to the journals and anthologies that published the following poems in the current or an earlier form:

Askew Poetry Journal: "Distances," first published as "On the Edge," "The Piano"
Atlanta Review: "Rescues," "Unnamed"
The Comstock Review: "Kindness," "Red Dog"
Hubbub: "Red Bricks"
Marin Poetry Center Anthology: "Chalk Drawings"
Original Weather (Uttered Chaos, 2011): "First Word"
Parabola: "Sacred Love," (Recipient of a Poetry of the Sacred, Thomas Merton Prize)
SOLO Voyage (Glenna Luschei, 2023): "My Hair Stylist"
Spillway: "Homeopathic Remedy"
VoiceCatcher: "Midnight Choices"
Women in a Golden State (Gunpowder Press, 2025): "Widows & Widowers"

Several poems first appeared in chapbooks:

Red Bricks (Fae Press, 2013): "Call & Response," "Chalk Drawings," "Isla Negra," "Red Bricks"

The Way of Stones (Finishing Line Press, 2009): "Inhaling Together" first published as "Hands of Pech Merle," "On the Beach," "Swish"

My long journey to the publication of this book has been filled with the luminous and the challenging. Fortunately, the journey has been blessed consistently with wonderful poets and friends who have inspired and supported me. My gratitude to all of them is deep and abiding.

To Robert Bly and Marion Woodman for a late-in-life initiation into poetry and to Thomas R. Smith for early mentoring.

To Lynn Ireland, Adrienne Amundsen, and Barbara McEnerney, my poetry group of Bay Area soul sisters who have been sharing lives and poems for more than twenty years. Special thanks to Barbara whose hand and heart touched every page in this collection. This book would not have come to fruition without her.

To my poetry friends in Eugene, Oregon: Claudia Lapp, Jenny Root, Denise Wallace, Laura LeHew, and the late Charles Thielman, and a shoutout to Scott Landfield of Tsunami Books for supporting the poetry community in Eugene.

To the poets who create the events, poems and books that make Ventura and the Central Coast of California a vibrant poetry community. In particular, my love to Anita McLaughlin for her enlivening and sweet friendship and to Marsha de la O for her many kindnesses to me. Grateful nods to Jennifer Kelley, Barbara Lipscomb, Phil Taggart, Friday Gretchen Treur, Sean Colletti, Mary Kay Rummel, Laure-Anne Bosselaar, and Ron Fullerton for their many contributions to the poetry world here. Finally, Glenna Luschei gave me a warm welcome when I first arrived in town and the regulars who attend the monthly open mic at Blanchard Library in Santa Paula bring joy into my life—Anita McLaughlin, Gale Naylor, John Gentry, Chuck Spink, Greg Lanner, Linda Derbyshire, and Teri Rhodehamel.

To my cherished friends who read parts of this collection: Wilma Friesema, Laurel Connell, Glori Zeltzer, and Marilee Stark, and to my sister Linda Villa and my stepdaughter Celeen Evans for unwavering support.

And to my late husband, Roger Barry. He may be in other realms but he is always present in the living waters of my life.

Contents

THE CREATIVE LIFE

First Word	17
Inhaling Together	18
Chalk Drawings	20
Call and Response	21
Sacred Love	22
Isla Negra	23
They Played On	25
Red Bricks	26

ROOTS

Midnight Choices	31
Waiting	32
Unnamed	33
Kindness	34
The Piano	35
The Bubble	37
Final Words	38
Homeopathic Remedy	39
What I Would Say	40
Southern Comforts	42

THE SEA

Coming Home	47
On the Beach	48
Jewels	49
Red Dog	50
Distances	51

Riptide and Solace	52
Canceled Tickets	53
It Could Have Been Different	54

LOVE AND LOSS

My Husband's Boots	57
First Seeds	58
Our Marriage	59
Nocturnal Messages	60
What a Dream Foretold	61
On Reopening	63
Rescues	65
My Hair Stylist	67
The Lives of a Screwdriver	68
Widows & Widowers	69
Ho'omaluhia	70

A WIDER LENS

Candles in the Night	75
The Luck of an Apple	76
Tree Medicine	78
Redemption	79
In Praise of My Arms	80
Still Tethered	81
Swish	82

Notes	85

THE CREATIVE LIFE

First Word

from the original hand it comes
stylus of sap and light
piercing sea's empty drift
bestowing a new alphabet

stylus of sap and light
into a basin of salted gas
bestowing a new alphabet
letters swirl in the sea

into a basin of salted gas
binding, wheeling apart
letters swirl in the sea
undreamed-of syllables

binding, wheeling apart
salt clots, proteins spark
undreamed-of syllables
first word of the deep

salt clots, proteins spark
a small eyeless creature appears
first word of the deep
from the original hand, it comes

Inhaling Together

Caves at Pech Merle, France

amidst swirling orange
dripstone and crimson arches
you're here

you lift a brush to dot
the horses' flanks
allow the wall to contour
their thick muscles

pressing your paint-coated
hands into the stone
you leave a spray of handprints—
small dark roses

some say you were a shaman
invoking the thunder of the bison
the winged fleetness of the horse

and maybe that explains
the magic here
you're as palpable
as the people beside me now

but there is something more
a sense that as you painted
your inner eye flew open
and you saw us—

tall strangers
from a distant future
standing before your walls
seeing you clearly

you seeing us seeing you
time slips its bindings
and we inhale together

Chalk Drawings

Unseen hands have left drawings
    on the bridge above the river—
        a fairy with streaming hair
and unfurled wings,
    a guitar marked Gibson,
        LS and PR forever.

I imagine the midnight artists,
    moonlight white as bone,
        the water's relentless flow.

The river asks of them,
    what gives meaning
        in this chilly hour?

Backs bent, fingers wrapped
    around sticks of peach and blue,
        they draw their answers,

as the ancient ones
    painted hands and horses
        on the limestone belly of earth.

Call and Response

for Judith Sparks
—Eugene, Oregon

without much fuss she labors
in her studio on a backstreet

on the walls
salmon mandalas
paper money with salmon imprints
salmon prayer flags

when young, she first heard
about the great orange fish
voyagers of rivers and sea

how they heave and strain
to climb the impassible
concrete of our dams

each year she imagines them
crying out as they fall back
and responds in the best way she knows

staining and painting
cutting and gluing
her hands shaping a prayer
      may you find your way home

Sacred Love

Ventura Beach

Manuel Cisneros built a crèche of rocks
    close to the lip of the sea.

Hundreds walked down to see
    Mary, Joseph, and the three wise men,
the small stone Jesus
    on his rock cradle.

Around them all, Manuel built
    a low mission wall,
no mortar or glue, just rocks
    coaxed and gentled together.

He called his sculpture Sacred Love,
    speaking of the story he told,

and love is what I call
    the work of his hands,
like that of the Tibetan monks
    who spend long weeks
  sifting colored sand,

and when their mandala is done,
    the monks sweep it away,
just like Manuel heads home
    when his work is done,

leaving the holy family alone
    to face the winds
        and the hungry sea.

Isla Negra

for Pablo Neruda

for decades he lived
next to the sea
collecting
shells and sea fruit
from unknowable reaches
listening
to the ceaseless surf

wooden figureheads
sailed through his rooms
maiden and queen
pirate and angel
salt-stained
ripped from the prows
of ships long gone

their hollowed eyes
remembering
how the sea rose up
in mountains
and masts pitched
like sticks in the wind

I can see the poet
buttering his toast
pouring his whiskey neat
and tossing it back

a man at ease
with these wraiths
and the sea's constant toll

his poems strong enough
to bear the cries
of such a place

They Played On

April 14. 1912

All eight were lost
>when the Titanic went down—

men with violins tucked
>under trembling chins,

cellists bowing strings
>wet from sweat and spray,

and the pianist who kept his fingers
>on the slick keys.

They faced the gaping mouth of the sea
>and played on.

Their music soothed those in boats,
>lowered into the black water,

calmed the abandoned ones,
>without lifeboats to save them.

Now as storms and fires ravage
>our overheated world,

I try to write a few good words
>and show some kindness.

I remember the eight who made music
>as their ship went down.

Red Bricks

Holland, 1944

Like a dream repeating,
hinting at a sea change needed,
his story pursues me.

Near the end of the war,
many countries have fallen,
crushed like fields of poppies.

A man is warned tanks are coming,
houses along his road
will be plowed to the ground.

This man takes apart his home,
brick by brick, hauling each one
by truck and cart to a far field,
then sends his children away.

After peace returns, he hauls back
his bricks, rebuilding his house
exactly as it was, and then brings
his children home.

How his story feeds this wanderer
who has lived in many places,
under many roofs.

Hard to imagine such close
knowing of each brick, its heft,
how it leans into and supports all others.
Hard to grasp a one and only home
lived in for a lifetime.

His red bricks shimmer now,
beckoning me to something deep-
rooted, perhaps first felt by early
men in rough caverns—

a love of home, its sheltering
embrace holding us
in chill wind and beneath
unfathomable skies.

ROOTS

Midnight Choices

I startle awake and a witch is crouched
        in the corner of my room,

yellow frizzed hair,
        her eyes hungry crows.

One mole rises from her chin
        like a dab of tar.

I'm three, her cackle echoes
        with murderous intent.

Small twitching girl,
        I scan my choices,

slide bare feet to the floor
        and creep toward Mother's bed,

a place already known
        to be cold as ice.

Waiting

She lies unmoving on her bed,
a cool cloth draped across her face.

When my mother lies so still,
I don't make a sound.

For hours, I gaze out at leafless trees,
the snow-laden earth,

watch for my father's brown hat,
his camel-hair coat,

wait for him to grow larger
as he strides up the street.

Until he returns, sadness seeps
into my bones,

my mother and I locked
        in the chilly embrace
of a Pittsburgh winter.

Unnamed

Post-War Pittsburgh

As if they had never been,
my family didn't speak of forced marches
or the murder of millions,
though the war was not long over,

and we lived in Squirrel Hill,
a neighborhood of synagogues and delis,
where loss stalked the streets
and no one had been spared.

At our table sat our own ghosts—
my mother's first love, killed in battle,
the boys my father flew with,
the ones who didn't come home.

Back then, we placed our trust in TV.
Robert Young assured us that fathers
know best, Donna Reed soothed
with her gingham, her satisfied smiles.

That's how it was—pastel appliances
washed away our stains, shiny
new cars drove us through darkness
that hovered and was never named.

Kindness

For years, I saw them through a scavenger's eye,
kind mothers in orange brick houses—
Mrs. Levy, Black, and Mendelsohn, smaller
and darker than my own mother, their homes
smelling of wet wool and chicken soup.

On weekends, I set out early and when doors
opened, they were there, offering quick hugs
before sending me upstairs to play.
At noon, feeding us kids thick dill pickles
and pastrami on rye.

Of their sorrows, I knew nothing—
arms tattooed with numbers, the dead
wandering our common streets. What
I knew and relied on—them treating me
like their own, until the last light faded
and it was time to head home.

The Piano

It stood by the brass spittoon
        in our hallway, an upright
wooden box, a dust catcher without a voice.

For a short time. my fingers lumbered
        across the keys. My sister played
a bit longer, then silence.

One day a teacher asked,
        does your father still play?

You've got it wrong, I told her.
        My mother puts on Mathis
at Christmas, Streisand at parties,
        there's no music in-between.

My teacher looked stunned, she herself
        had trained that promising boy,
a concert hall in his future.

When asked, my father denied it.
        I pressed and he finally spat out
eight words, hard as stone: *I was going
        nowhere, a weak left hand.*

We never spoke of it again
        but I have often wondered
how his music vanished,
        leaving no trace.

Maybe it happened in a B-24,
        staccato gunfire rending the air,
his quick hands clutching a bombsight,

perhaps when he dropped bombs,
        and cities burned, a part
of him, more delicately wired,
        closed down forever.

Or maybe it wasn't like that at all.
        Only this is certain—
a piano-playing boy went to war
        and he never returned.

The Bubble

We barrel down the road
in our red Country Squire—
Dad at the wheel looking like Cary Grant,
Mother as beautiful as the actress
who left Hollywood to marry a prince.

The three of us kids, squirming
in the back seat, sing camp songs:
a hundred bottles of beer on the wall,
a hundred bottles of beer, take one down
and pass it around, ninety-nine bottles
of beer on the wall . . .

I see Mother clearly—she unwraps
ham sandwiches from waxed paper,
rolls down the window and tosses out
the paper, followed later by napkins
and Dixie cups. Debris unfurls
behind us like banners in the wind.

It's the fifties and like the red-winged horse
at the gas pump, we're lifting above
the earth. Elves will spirit away litter,
gas tanks will always be full.

It's a bright day in the bubble.
The sun shines like a gold coin
and we're flying high.

Final Words

She sits next to her husband of fifty years,
cancer and chemo have almost
completed their two-step.

Her face, eaten away over time,
resembles a bird's but her hair surprises
with new red, brown, and silver threads.

She and her husband are drinking
their evening wine, one of the civilities
they have staked their lives on.

He, who in earlier days, perhaps
touched her less than she wished,
now runs his fingers through her hair.

Isn't this beautiful? he asks.
Who could believe such colors?
A master's palette.

She isn't exactly sure where she is,
yet sits straight in her chair,
takes slow sips of wine.

Homeopathic Remedy

part woman, part bird
you stretch your ruined face
into a smile

hold out a hand
dry as a November leaf

thank you for coming today,
you say to the medic
come to take you

that was the day before you died
the small stone in your breast
spread to eyes, bones, liver

now the same stone is in my breast

and I who rarely
      sought your help

slip memories of your final grace
under my tongue
rub them into my wrist

mama, I whisper,
      give me strength

What I Would Say

to Grace Braun Ridall, (1926–1996)

Sometimes, Mother, I wish
I could teleport back and help you
through our early days together. You lying
on the bed day after day, a cool cloth
across your forehead, and me tiptoeing
around you, quiet as a cat. Already at three,
understanding how quickly the chill
of ice can turn to burning steam.

I would rock you and whisper, *I know.*
I know the boy you loved went to war
and didn't come back and how no living man
could compete with that untested love.
Certainly not my father, a handsome soldier
with his own pack of troubles.

I would say to you, *I know.*
I have read your journals and I know
you pieced yourself together after
your first love died and you went east
to college, first girl in a small town outside
Pittsburgh to break into the Ivy League.
Your pages shimmer with hope.

I would say, *I know*—just as you graduated
and were about to step out into the big life
your college promised you, the boys returned
from war, and, like Rosie the Riveter,
you were handed an apron you couldn't refuse.

But mostly I would name the terrible truth
between us—mothering didn't come easily
to you. My first cry was the death knell
of your dreams. How could you not take
to your bed, the sound of closing doors
slamming through you?

I would massage your temples,
and say, *don't add guilt to your burdens.*
It is true, for many years I wrestled with how
my early days warped my own heart.
I fled everything reminding me of you.

But I would assure you, over time,
grief and rage have settled like sediment
in a river, and now, I can honor you
as first word, primal material, the moist
clay from which I have shaped
a life I can call my own.

Southern Comforts

for my grandmother, Anice Daniels Ridall (1897–1969)

It would be a day like this one,
fog low-hanging and the veil slightly parted,
when you'd at last stop by.

We'd marvel at one another,
both of us gray now, and you'd wonder
what happened to the restless girl
with her long blond hair.

I'd tell you I traveled to California
with its snaking coastline of cliffs and sand,
and settled in as if I was made
for life there.

I'd ask you about the things
I didn't think about when
I was still a girl.

Did you regret leaving the South
for a handsome Yankee, both drinker
and gambler, and did the chillier North
ever feel like your home?

I'd let you know I remember
how your skin smelled of roses,
and can still taste your spice cakes and hams,
your sweet tea that slaked my thirst.

But what mattered most was this—
you noticed my mother
was harsh.

You naming what no one else
seemed to see steadied a lurching girl.
You caught me in your arms
as I was falling.

THE SEA

Coming Home

Coming to California
as a drifting girl,
the sea welcomed me.

The unbounded blue ripples,
the wide unobstructed sky called me
to seek out my own far horizons.
The rhythm of waves breaking
was like a mother's heartbeat
and I was soothed.

On a spring morning,
a whale arose a few feet from shore.
She stayed beside me as I walked
down the beach, watching me
with one great dark eye.

In my new town, strangers
seemed oddly familiar, something
kindred drawing us to a freethinking
place at the edge of a continent.

Coming to California,
my dangling roots slid into the earth
and I began to make a life,

never far from the briny
comforts of the sea, never far
from the people and stories
I encountered there.

On the Beach

he's nine or ten
all freckles and knobs

a bit of a wizard
he conjures moats and turrets
from wet grit

works fast
fueled by an unseen wave
he knows is coming

he's old enough
to know his labor
perches on a fragile edge

it will be years
before he understands
this is his life

Jewels

for Wilma

Toes pointed toward the clouds,
she and I chat as we float
on the glistening jade sea.

The water ripples—
a tortoise-shelled dome followed
by a mottled head with onyx eyes
arises between us.

We two friends become three,
for a fleeting moment swaying together,
cradled beneath a topaz-blue sky

Red Dog

Again and again, the dog leapt into the surf,
his wet fur burnished copper,
his eyes sea-lit and intent.

Like a deer over a low hedge,
he arced easily over crests of waves
before paddling back to shore.

He had no time for people
or other dogs on that beach,
it was just him and the wide rolling water.

As a seeker longs for the touch of a holy man,
I followed the red dog from Surfer's Point
down to Ventura Pier,

wanting the blessing of that shining creature,
to touch his coat ever so briefly as he ran
in and out of the blue September sea.

Distances

No more than two years old,
his body packed in a small wetsuit,
he watches his mother and father
who have paddled out
to where the waves break.

His eyes are as locked onto them
as theirs are onto the horizon.
A teenage sitter tries to distract him—
he will have none of it.

The cold water is gnawing on his toes
but he stands as stubborn as stone,
on a Sunday morning at the edge
of an impassable sea.

Riptide and Solace

Backpack stuffed with chocolate and socks,
he marched out into the world. He was just three,
a small warrior with a brown dog, both of them
in search of a safe place.

When a stranger returned him home, he endured
long years before he could leave for good.

I met him after his black hair had turned grey
and he had retired from decades as a cop, fighting
relentless crime in a large American city.

His kids, who had the childhood he never had,
were grown, and his wife was gone too.

He talked to me of cops living at the margins,
an old dog as their only companion, of ancient times
when soldiers, returning home from battle,
lived outside the city gates.

He thought the stain of blood created this distance,
but I thought it might be a warrior's eyes, like his own,
unsettling with dark knowledge and a faraway stare.

I see him often now, walking down by Surfer's Point,
a red boxer by his side. He's at home with the sea
and its entwined truths of riptide and solace.

Canceled Tickets

Second Santa Barbara Oil Spill

They were out that day,
three hundred dolphins jumping
in parallel arches, the sea a milky churn.

For an hour they played near us,
almost grazing our hull. Our sunburned
faces stretched into smiles.

We clicked our cameras, and maybe
some of us imagined swimming
beside them in the living water,
our dying world redeemed.

Soon after, the news came—
a burst pipe, sludge and stink
pouring into the same water
where the dolphins swam.

How to face those joyful creatures?
I make plans to visit them,
but no longer believe we deserve
such pleasure.

I buy and cancel tickets,
over and over again.

It Could Have Been Different

Miles of glossy furrows
viewed from a sun-lit beach
in a town as safe as any place
on our perilous planet.

It could have been different.
I might have been an African man,
snatched from home, trapped
for months in the filth of a ship's hold,

or a whaler chasing a humpback
along the path of her yearly travels,
the sea a pitiless place.

I might have been a mother
in an overfull boat, fleeing guns
and hunger, the sea about to swallow
my cold and frightened child.

I don't know who spins
the great wheel. I only know
the gift of sitting here, my hair
lifting in the breeze, warm sand
spilling through my cupped fingers.

LOVE AND LOSS

My Husband's Boots

stand by his chair in the pale morning sun,
camo green and brown
with thick tread and leather laces,

akin to another pair that carried him
between burning trees and bleeding men,
held him firm during long still hours
when a soldier's nerves were frayed.

My husband has been away
from the jungle for decades now,
we live a quiet life in a quiet town,

but his boots speak of an earlier time,
of how he was both broken and grew strong,
of a life forged long ago in the lush
murderous green.

First Seeds

To not wield words as weapons
and to remember how easy
it is to harm a human heart.

These are vows you and I made
when the world was on fire with new love
and we were weaving our lives together.

And we have kept to these things,
even when we are bruised
by the storms between us.

From the start, I have rested my head
on your chest each night, even when
it cost me to cross cold sheets,

and you have wrapped me in your arms,
even when you longed to shield
your own aching.

Our first seeds, faithfully tended,
until love is now guarded by a stand
of tall leafy trees.

Our Marriage

the Rainforest, Peru

You, once a soldier in a jungle war,
yearn for the emerald canopy, the jazz
of rain on broad leaves. You say,
Let's go to the Amazon.

I, a city girl who hates humidity
and yet wants to please, say *No,
I wish I could, but no.* I think
I've shut that door.

Months pass. Banana leaves,
big as boats, drift through my dreams.
From the corner of my eyes,
I see parrots lift their bright wings.

More months and here we are amidst
sprawling ferns and sixty-foot vines,
the air pulsing with sounds
of monkeys, mosquitos, and macaws.

Sweat courses down my breasts
and I can barely speak. When a sloth
wraps her arms around my neck,
she's like a lost child come home.

That's how it is—yin and yang,
flint on stone, a chafing that sparks
undreamed-of worlds. I reach across
the divide and choose you,
again and again.

Nocturnal Messages

while you sleep
your fingers make their way
toward me
across the warm sheets

they tap on my belly
then settle between my breasts
like five kittens
curled together

when daybreak comes
your fingers will pick up
a coffee cup and press down
on computer keys

they won't remember
how they came to me
when the world was dark
and silent

What a Dream Foretold

Everything was as clear
        as my hand before me now,
the earth shaking like a ragdoll
        in a madman's hands,
infernos raging
        on every ridgeline.

I saw a tsunami pull
        a river out to sea, sweeping
screaming bathers away.

When a little girl in a red dress
        and a small white dog crossed
my path, grit cut through terror.

I would lead these two
        up the mountain, find refuge
for them in a world filled
        with smoke and ruin.

I should have known
        this dream was about more
than surviving a pandemic,
        about even more than facing
the firestorms and floods ripping
        across our world.

But I didn't know,
        and when you died,
I fell to the ground,
        without words or belief,
as if I hadn't been warned of
        my own apocalypse coming.

On Reopening

At the pool, kids squeal
and splash in warm water,
not so long ago forbidden.

One of my friends hugs
a plump toddler, a granddaughter
whose infancy she missed.

Another buys a ticket
to the vineyard in Tuscany
she has yearned for.

Masks are coming off
and people are jumping aboard
the freedom train.

I remember when you drove
to the old Toys R Us for your first shot.
You waited in line for hours.

When you returned home,
you were pale and unsteady,
wondered why you were so tired.

Three weeks later you were tireder still
and I drove you for the second shot,
the one we believed would save you.

We never guessed, while we were
avoiding Covid, death was stalking
us from another direction.

I never guessed—when
the train barreled out of the tunnel,
you would be gone,
and the world I loved
would never reopen again.

Rescues

Some people said I was kind
        to rescue the little white dog.
It never felt that way. Soft
        tawny ears, smart brown eyes,
I was hers from the start.

Eva did have issues. Being dumped
        on a city street, her small body
stuffed with pups, her milky teats dragging
        across the pavement, marked her.

For months, she tracked my every
        move, shaking and screaming
like a creature on fire. She needed special care
        but then, so did we.

Knowing nothing of the virus
        shutting us in, Eva danced about
on hind legs, raced through
        the house, making us laugh.

The days grew longer. Fewer
        people were dying on machines
with masked strangers by their side.
        My husband sat in his chair,
headed toward his own end.

I tucked quilts around him
        and Eva sat on his lap, hour
after hour, keeping him company,
        keeping him warm.

Tonight, like every night now,
        Eva will curl up against my belly,
her eyelids twitching as she
        follows her dreams

I'll stroke the hollow space
        where my husband once lay,
tell him of the happenings
        of this day that has passed.

My Hair Stylist

says my hair is thinner.
Her small clever fingers
lift a clump of short strands
and she adds, "Maybe these
hairs are falling out or maybe
this is new growth." She's
being diplomatic. In a year
when one coast burns while
the other is underwater, when
thousands die because too many
insist on their god-given right
to live unmasked and when
my husband takes his last
breath and his absence is an
unseen beast feeding on my
heart, in a year such as this,
the body speaks truth
in any way it can.

The Lives of a Screwdriver

My husband's screwdriver resides
now in Casciana Alta in the Tuscan hills.
Sitting on a sill, it awaits its next task.

A Black & Decker special, it shines
with oils from my husband's hands,
always fixing what was broken.

After he died, it lay in his vacated garage.
I searched for who would use it best,
feared I could never release it.

Now it begins anew with a friend
who is starting over across the sea.
In this, it may be a beacon.

One day I too may look out at light
falling on new vistas, may learn
to love my life once again.

Widows & Widowers

Those early days and months
    in the caves of sorrow,
a cold bed that burns the skin,
    long silences broken
by conversations with the dead.

A time when scamsters call
    to cheat a grief-addled brain,
and when appliances break down
    and cars refuse to start—
a curious mirroring of the heart's
    unraveling.

Many stories are heard—
    a man who sleeps in a La-Z-Boy,
unable to bear his wife's scent
    lingering in the sheets,
a woman who sleeps on the edge
    of a mattress, still offering
a dead husband more than his fair share.

Stories about the ones who can't eat
    and those who eat too much,
those who hole up alone for months
    and those at the Justice of the Peace,
their last spouse barely in the ground.

Stories both unique and the same—
    a club for the broken-hearted
        no one wants to join.

Ho'omaluhia

Kāne'ohe, Hawai'i

When you asked me to bring
your ashes to Hoʻomaluhia,
I wasn't surprised.

You, my jungle-loving soldier,
raised to manhood beneath
the triple canopy of Vietnam,
the ground bursting with life,
even amidst the ravages of war.

The thick flows of sap offered you
the milk your mother never did
and in the jungle's throb, you first heard
the heart of our earth beating.

Fathering came to you there too—
a stern call to rise above aches
and dread, to channel fear into action
when battle cries pierced
the lush jungle brush.

You, my jungle-loving soldier,
who arrived in Nam an unsteady boy
and left a man who knew how to stand
firm, a man with some wounds
that would heal and others
that never would.

When you asked me to bring
your remains to a place akin to Nam,
it came as no surprise.

You trusted the tangle of fern
and frond, the moist green earth
to hold you close and lead you on
your journey's next steps.

A WIDER LENS

Candles in the Night

In the caves of sorrow,
we soon learn it's not just death
over which we have no sway.

We may yearn for renewal
but it's as distant as our loved one
who has left this world.

We can try to shorten
the slow ways of grief—
spending time with people who offer
comfort, performing the tasks
of mooring a life,

or pore over the words
of poets and saints in search
of the light that eludes us.

We can do these things
but this is what we learn—
the unfreezing of a heart,
the yearned-for flows of new life
are beyond our grasp.

At the end of our efforts,
we bow low before a mystery
that can never be forced.

We reach out our hands
like cups, like question marks,
like candles in the night.

The Luck of an Apple

How kindly the warm hands
of my bath wash away grit,
loosen the body's tight knots,

while in Gaza, women lift
cups of dirty water to the parched
lips of their children. Choosing
between disease and certain death,
there is but one choice.

In a few days, I will lie safely
numbed in a clean white room.
A surgeon will remove a dark spot
from my left breast,

as hundreds of Gazan women
huddle together in hospitals.
Moans of the maimed and dying
fill the fragile sanctuaries.
Painkillers are as elusive as peace.

I don't know why life offers
its gifts with such an uneven hand.

And please don't speak of
past lives and karma or heavenly gates
that will fly open to redeem
the injustice of this world.

Shouldn't we cringe at using
such beliefs to help us sleep?

A woman walks by a tree
just as an apple drops.
She scoops it up and takes a bite,
her cares calmed by a burst
of needed sweetness.

Another woman stares
at scorched earth. She pushes
on, beyond hope for relief
or for the luck of an apple
falling from a tree.

Tree Medicine

What if we could release a few lines
of our human story of being bounded
and alone, and instead meditated
on trees lifting their hallelujah arms
into the light that feeds them?

Or if we heeded the hidden life
of trees—their unseen exchanges
with the spongy creatures of the dark,
with the snaking roots of their neighbors?

Trees cannot write treatises
about how the world works
or poems about how it feels to live
a beautiful and perilous life,

but they know how to stand
firm for centuries, giving and taking,
so the earth can thrive. They know
a holy conversation we humans
are struggling to join.

Redemption

Singapore is planting trees
everywhere.

In new parks and green belts,
on narrow balconies
and rising rooftops.

Trees offering leafy parasols
for the baking earth, vapor
to cool hot murderous air.

This small island of concrete
and commerce shows us
how to redeem our calloused hearts,

how to heal the plundering
and polluting that hurl us
toward oblivion.

In Praise of My Arms

My long simian arms,
faithful sidekicks
that ride by my side,

without your knobby hinges
opening wide and swinging outward,
my desires couldn't shape
the moist clay of this world.

Your ten digits push
and pull, peel and dice,
have guided my pen over the peaks
and through the valleys
of the blank page.

At other times, your versatile hinges
close and you curve inward,
allowing me to embrace a friend,

or to bring a lover nearer and nearer,
until distance disappears
and my lover and I vanish
for a moment, one into the other.

Still Tethered

Call me
a wind-bitten shack
on a beach's shifting sands,
or a weathered kite,
still tethered here,
still awaiting my next updraft.

So much has been lost
on the way—a young body
leaping and twirling in open seas,

my book-of-lifers,
that irreplaceable pod,
many swimming now beyond
the last known horizon.

My tale is almost told,
girl to woman to elder—

the meetings
(were they chance or fate?)
that opened just the right doors,

the storms I thought
I would never survive but life
would not be denied.

The arc of my life is now in focus
and shared with friends,
our stories and hard-earned truths
shimmer like golden fish
in the living waters between us.

Swish

a fish tail finning
through a pond's
dark waters

a skirt stroking
a woman's thighs
as wind sweeps down
the street

swish, the back and forth
of a cat's tail
a pendulum metering
a small bird's last moments

decades caressing us
bruising us
as they blow by

swish
our final breath inhaled
by the waiting sky

Notes

"First Word" is an ekphrastic poem based on "Basin 16," a mixed media drawing by Robert Tomlinson, formerly of Oregon.

"Red Bricks" is based on a story told to me by Wilma Friesema. Her grandfather, Willem Vander Kooy of Rotterdam dismantled his family home and carted the bricks away before German troops razed his neighborhood. After World War II ended, he returned his bricks back to his property and rebuilt his home, exactly as it had been before.

"Still Tethered" is an ekphrastic poem based on "Tethered," a pen and ink drawing by Anita McLaughlin of Santa Paula, California.

About the Author

Kathryn Ridall, a poet and nonfiction writer, was born and raised in Pittsburgh, Pennsylvania and moved to California in her twenties. She has published three chapbooks and two poetry anthologies as well as the award-winning prose book, *Dreaming at the Gates: How Dreams Guide.* For several years, she was the editor and publisher of Fae Press, a small press in Eugene that published Oregon poets.

Kathryn has worked in the mental health field since she was nineteen. Her writing and her work as a psychotherapist are the two wings of her creative life. She lives in Ventura, California.

www.ingramcontent.com/pod-product-compliance
Lightning Source LLC
Chambersburg PA
CBHW070938160426
43193CB00011B/1730